# LAKE CLASSICS

### *Great American Short Stories II*

❧❧❧

# Charlotte Perkins GILMAN

Stories retold by Emily Hutchinson
Illustrated by James Balkovek

**LAKE EDUCATION**
Belmont, California

# LAKE CLASSICS

### Great American Short Stories I

Washington Irving, Nathaniel Hawthorne, Mark Twain, Bret Harte, Edgar Allan Poe, Kate Chopin, Willa Cather, Sarah Orne Jewett, Sherwood Anderson, Charles W. Chesnutt

### Great American Short Stories II

Herman Melville, Stephen Crane, Ambrose Bierce, Jack London, Edith Wharton, Charlotte Perkins Gilman, Frank R. Stockton, Hamlin Garland, O. Henry, Richard Harding Davis

### Great British and Irish Short Stories

Arthur Conan Doyle, Saki (H. H. Munro), Rudyard Kipling, Katherine Mansfield, Thomas Hardy, E. M. Forster, Robert Louis Stevenson, H. G. Wells, John Galsworthy, James Joyce

### Great Short Stories from Around the World

Guy de Maupassant, Anton Chekhov, Leo Tolstoy, Selma Lagerlöf, Alphonse Daudet, Mori Ogwai, Leopoldo Alas, Rabindranath Tagore, Fyodor Dostoevsky, Honoré de Balzac

Cover and Text Designer: Diann Abbott

Library of Congress Catalog Number: 94-075027
ISBN 1-56103-019-8
Printed in the United States of America
1 9 8 7 6 5 4 3 2 1

# CONTENTS

# ❦ Lake Classic Short Stories ❦

*"The universe is made of stories, not atoms."*

—Muriel Rukeyser

*"The story's about you."*

—Horace

Everyone loves a good story. It is hard to think of a friendlier introduction to classic literature. For one thing, short stories are *short*—quick to get into and easy to finish. Of all the literary forms, the short story is the least intimidating and the most approachable.

Great literature is an important part of our human heritage. In the belief that this heritage belongs to everyone, *Lake Classic Short Stories* are adapted for today's readers. Lengthy sentences and paragraphs are shortened. Archaic words are replaced. Modern punctuation and spellings are used. Many of the longer stories are abridged. In all the stories, painstaking care has been taken to preserve the author's unique voice.

*Lake Classic Short Stories* have something for everyone. The hundreds of stories in the collection cover a broad terrain of themes, story types, and styles. Literary merit was a deciding factor in story selection. But no story was included unless it was as enjoyable as it was instructive. And special priority was given to stories that shine light on the human condition.

Each book in the *Lake Classic Short Stories* is devoted to the work of a single author. Little-known stories of merit are included with famous old favorites. Taken as a whole, the collected authors and stories make up a rich and diverse sampler of the story-teller's art.

*Lake Classic Short Stories* guarantee a great reading experience. Readers who look for common interests, concerns, and experiences are sure to find them. Readers who bring their own gifts of perception and appreciation to the stories will be doubly rewarded.

# ❦ Charlotte Perkins Gilman ❧
## (1860–1935)

## About the Author

Charlotte Anna Perkins was born the year before the Civil War began. She died on the eve of World War II. Her father deserted his family shortly after she was born. After that he took little interest in Charlotte, other than to recommend books for her to read. Her first job as an adult was designing greeting cards. She began to write fiction at about the same time.

At age 24, she married an artist. After the birth of their child, a daughter, she suffered a severe depression. The doctor who treated her prescribed "as domestic a life as possible." He said that she should "never touch pen, brush, or pencil again." She used this experience as background for her masterpiece, *The Yellow Wallpaper.*

She moved to California with her daughter and divorced her husband. She was criticized by the press when her ex-husband and his second wife later shared custody of her daughter. After that, she began writing and lecturing about women's rights. She felt that women's financial dependence on men was not healthy either for men or for women. If women had more productive lives, she said, everyone would be better off.

In 1900, she married her first cousin, a man who shared her views. When he died suddenly in 1934, she moved to Pasadena, California, to live with her daughter. Ill with cancer and thinking that her active life was over, she committed suicide in 1935.

Charlotte Perkins Gilman had shocking ideas for her times. Today, those ideas are accepted by most reasonable people. If you're interested in stories about women who refuse to accept narrow lives, you'll like Charlotte Perkins Gilman.

# The Yellow Wallpaper

How much control should anyone have over another person's life? This is the story of a trapped woman who struggles to escape. Why is it that no one around her can see what she sees? This moving story—and its powerful social message—made its author famous all over the world.

THERE ARE THINGS IN THE WALLPAPER THAT NOBODY
KNOWS ABOUT BUT ME. AND THEY WILL NEVER KNOW.

# The Yellow Wallpaper

John has rented us a beautiful old house for the summer. I think it might be haunted. If not, why would it be so cheap? John laughs at me, of course—but one expects that in marriage.

John is a doctor. Sometimes I think that is one reason I don't get well faster. Of course, I wouldn't say that aloud to a living soul. But it feels good just to write this thought on dead paper.

You see, John does not believe that I am sick! He says the only thing wrong with me is a little problem with my nerves. What is one to do? If a doctor of high standing—who is even one's own husband—says this, what is one to do?

My brother is also a doctor. He is also of high standing. And he says the same thing.

So I do what they say. I am absolutely forbidden to "work" until I am well again.

Personally, I don't think they are right.

Personally, I believe that all the excitement and change of work would do me a world of good.

But what is one to do?

I sometimes think that it would be better, in my condition, if I had more to do. But John says that the very *worst* thing I can do is to think about my condition. So I will let it alone and talk about the house.

It is the most beautiful place! Around the grounds there are hedges and walls and gates that lock. And there are lots of little houses for the gardeners and other workers.

There is a *delicious* garden! I never saw such a garden. It is large and shady, full of paths and benches.

But as beautiful and wonderful as it is, there is something strange about the house. I can feel it.

I don't like our room a bit. I wanted a room downstairs that opened on the garden. Roses climbed all over the window of that room. But John would not hear of it.

I have a set schedule for each hour of the day. John makes sure I have nothing to worry about. He said we came here just for me. I was to have perfect rest, he said, and all the air I could get.

The room at the top of the house is big and airy. It takes up almost the whole floor. It has windows that open in all directions, to let in lots of fresh air and sunshine. I think it was a baby's room first. Then it must have been a playroom after that, and later a gym. I say that because the windows have bars on them to protect little children. There are also rings and things in the walls.

The paint and wallpaper look as if rough boys lived in this room. The paper is stripped off in big patches all around the head of my bed. It is stripped off about as far as I can reach. On the other side of the room it is also stripped off in a big place near the floor. I never saw a worse wallpaper in my life.

The color is awful, almost sickening. It is a dirty yellow, strangely faded by the sunlight. No wonder the boys who stayed here hated it! I would hate it myself if I had to live in this room very long.

Ah! Here comes John, and I must put this away. He hates to have me write a word.

\* \* \*

We have been here two weeks. John is away all day. He is even away some nights when his cases are serious.

I am glad my case is not serious!

But these problems with my nerves are quite depressing. John does not know how much I really suffer.

Nobody would believe just how hard it is to do the little bit that I can do. Just to get dressed and talk to people—even that is hard.

I am glad Mary is so good with the baby. Such a dear baby! And yet I *cannot* be with him. It makes me so nervous.

I suppose John was never nervous in his life. He laughs at me so about not liking the wallpaper!

At first he promised to change the yellow paper on the walls. But later he said that I was letting it get the better of me. He said that nothing was worse for a nervous patient than to give in to such small things.

He said that after the wallpaper was changed, it would be one thing after another. Next it would be the heavy bed I didn't like. Then it would be the barred windows. Then it would be that gate at the head of the stairs, and so on.

"You know this place is doing you good," he said.

"Do let us go downstairs then," I said. "There are such pretty rooms there."

Then he took me in his arms and called me a blessed little goose. I suppose he is right about the beds and windows and all.

I suppose this is as nice a room as anyone could want. Out of one window I can see the garden. Out of another I can see the bay and a private dock. There is a beautiful road that goes from there to the house. I often think that I see people walking in the garden and down the many paths. But John says that I am just being silly. He says I should try to control my imagination. So I try.

I think sometimes that if I could only do my writing, I would feel better.

It is so discouraging not to have anyone to talk to about my work. When I get really well, John says we will ask Cousin Henry and Julia over to visit. But he says they would be too much for me right now.

I wish I could get well faster.

But I must not think about that. This wallpaper looks to me as if it *knew* what a bad influence it is!

Did I already say that the wallpaper is torn off in spots? The plaster itself is dug out of the wall here and there. And this big heavy bed looks as if it has been through the wars.

But I don't mind it a bit—only the paper.

There comes John's sister, Jennie. She is such a dear girl! I must not let her find me writing.

She is very good at taking care of the house. She doesn't even *want* to do anything else. In her mind, there is no better profession. I truly believe that she thinks it is the writing that made me sick!

But I can write when she is out. I can see her a long way off from these windows.

This wallpaper has another design under the first one. The design is in a different color. It is very annoying, for you can see it only in certain lights. Even then, it is not clear.

But in the places where the paper isn't faded, and where the light is just right, I can see *something*. There seems to be a strange sort of figure behind that silly front design.

There's sister on the stairs!

\* \* \*

Well, the Fourth of July is over! The guests are all gone, and I am so tired out. John thought it might do me good to see a little company. So we have just had mother and Nellie and the children down for a week.

Of course I didn't do a thing. Jennie sees to everything now.

But it made me tired all the same.

I cry at nothing—and I cry most of the time.

Of course I never cry when John is here, or anybody else. I cry only when I am alone.

And I am alone a good deal just now. John is kept in town very often by serious cases. His sister Jennie is good. She leaves me alone when I want her to.

So I walk a little in the garden or down the road. Sometimes I sit on the porch under the roses, or lie up here on my bed.

I'm getting to really like the room in spite of the wallpaper. Maybe it's *because* of the wallpaper.

It's on my mind so much!

I do know something about good design. I know this wallpaper was not designed well. It makes me tired to look at it. I will take a nap, I guess.

* * *

I don't know why I should write this.

I don't want to.

I don't feel able.

And I know John would think it was foolish. But I *must* say what I feel and think in some way. It is such a relief!

John says I must not lose my strength. He has me take cod liver oil and lots of tonics and things. He also has me take ale and wine and rare meat.

Dear John! He loves me very dearly, and hates to have me sick. I talked to him the other day. I told him how much I wish he would let me go visit Cousin Henry and Julia.

But he said I wasn't able to go. I did not make a good case for myself, for I was crying the whole time.

But then dear John took me in his arms and carried me upstairs. He put me on the bed and read to me until I was tired.

He said I was his darling and all he had. He said I must take care of myself for his sake, and try to get well.

John says that no one but myself can help me out of this illness. There's one good thing. I know the baby is well and happy. And he does not have to live in this room with this awful wallpaper.

If we had not used this room, that blessed child might have been put here! What a lucky escape for him! Why, I wouldn't have a child of mine live in such a room for anything!

I never thought of it before, but it is lucky that John put me in this room after all. I can stand it so much better than a baby could, you see.

Of course, I never talk about the wallpaper to them anymore. I have learned not to do that. But I keep watching it all the same.

There are things in the wallpaper that nobody knows about but me. And they never will know.

Behind that outside pattern, the dim shapes get clearer every day. They are always the same, only there are a lot more of them.

It looks like a woman is stooping down and creeping about behind that pattern. I don't like it a bit. I wonder—I begin to think—I wish John would take me away from here!

* * *

It is so hard to talk with John about my case. Of course that is because he is so wise, and because he loves me so.

But I tried it last night.

John was asleep and I hated to wake him up. So I kept still for a long time. I watched the moonlight on that wallpaper till I felt creepy.

The faint figure in the background seemed to shake the pattern on the wallpaper. It was as if she wanted to get out.

I got up softly and went to see if the paper *did* move. When I came back to bed, John was awake. "What is it, little girl?" he said. "Don't go walking about like that. You'll get cold."

I thought it was a good time to talk. So I told him that I really wasn't getting better here. I said I wished he would take me away.

"Why, darling!" said he. "Our lease will be up in three weeks. I don't see how we can leave before that. Of course—if you were in any danger—we would leave right away. But you really are better, dear, whether you can see it or not. I am a doctor, sweet wife, and I know. Your color is better, and so is your appetite."

"My appetite may be better in the evening with you here. But it's worse in the morning when you are away!"

"Bless her little heart!" he said, with a big hug. "She shall be as sick as she pleases! But now let's go back to sleep, and talk about it in the morning."

So of course I said nothing more. John went to sleep before long. He thought I was asleep first, but I wasn't. I lay there awake for hours. I was trying to decide whether the front pattern and the back pattern were moving together or separately.

\* \* \*

The pattern is really terrible. The color is bad enough, but the pattern is worse. It is like a bad dream.

There is one strange thing about this paper, a thing that nobody but me seems to notice. That is—it changes as the light changes.

When the sun comes in through the east window, it changes very quickly. In fact, I can never quite believe it.

That is why I always watch it.

By moonlight, I wouldn't even know it was the same paper.

At night, the design becomes bars. The outside pattern, I mean. The woman behind it is as plain as can be.

For a long time I was not sure what the thing behind the pattern really was. But now I am quite sure it is a woman.

By daylight, she is quiet and still. I think it is the outside pattern that keeps her so still. It is puzzling. Just wondering about it keeps me quiet by the hour.

I lie down ever so much now. John says it is good for me. He says I should sleep all I can. Indeed, he started the habit by making me lie down for an hour after each meal.

It is a very bad habit, I am sure. You see, I *don't* sleep. And that makes me lie to them, for I cannot tell them I'm awake. Oh, no!

The fact is, I am becoming afraid of John.

He seems very strange sometimes. Even his sister Jennie has a strange look.

It strikes me sometimes that perhaps it is the paper! I have watched John when he didn't know I was looking. Several times I have caught him *looking at the paper.* And Jennie, too. I caught Jennie with her hand on it once.

She didn't know I was in the room. When I asked her what she was doing with the paper, she turned around. She looked as if she had been caught stealing. Then she said that the paper stained everything it touched. She said that she had found yellow marks on all my clothes. She said she wished I would be more careful!

Didn't that sound innocent? But I *know* that she was studying that pattern. I don't want anyone to find out about it but myself!

*  *  *

Life is much more exciting now than it used to be. You see, I have something to look forward to—to watch. I really do eat better, and I am quieter than I was.

John is so pleased to see me getting better. He laughed a little the other day. He said I seemed to be getting better in spite of the awful wallpaper.

I laughed. I didn't want to tell him it was *because* of the wallpaper. I knew he would make fun of me. He might even want to take me away.

I don't want to leave now. I *can't* leave until I have found out about the paper. We still have a week to go, and I think that will be enough.

*  *  *

I'm feeling so much better!

I don't sleep much at night, because it is so interesting to watch the wallpaper. But I sleep a good deal in the daytime.

It is the strangest yellow, that wallpaper! It makes me think of all the yellow things I ever saw. I don't think of beautiful things like buttercups, but old, foul, bad yellow things.

And there is something else about that paper—the smell! I noticed it the very moment we came into the room. But with so much air and sun, the smell was not so strong. Now we have had a week of fog and rain, and the windows have been closed. But whether the windows are open or closed, the smell is always there.

It creeps all over the house.

I find it in the dining room, in the hall, and lying in wait for me on the stairs.

It gets into my hair.

Such a strange odor, too. I have spent hours trying to figure out just what it smells like. The only thing I can think of is that it is like the *color* of the paper. It is a yellow smell.

There is a very funny mark on this wall—low down, near the floor. The mark runs around the room. It goes behind every piece of furniture, except the bed.

It is a long, straight, even mark. It looks as if it had been rubbed over and over.

I wonder how it was done and who did it, and why. Round and round and round—round and round and round—it makes me dizzy!

* * *

I have discovered something important at last.

The front pattern *does* move—and no wonder! The woman in back of the pattern is shaking it!

Sometimes I think there are many women behind. Sometimes I think there is only one—but she crawls around fast. Her crawling shakes it all over.

In the very bright spots on the wallpaper, she keeps still. But in the very shady spots, she takes hold of the bars and shakes them hard.

All the time, of course, *she is trying to climb through.* But nobody could climb through that pattern.

* * *

I think that woman gets out in the daytime! And I'll tell you why, just between us. *I've seen her!* I can see her out of every one of my windows.

It is the woman in the wallpaper, I know, for she is always creeping. Most women do not creep by daylight.

I see her on that long road under the trees, just creeping along. When a carriage comes, she hides under the blackberry vines.

I don't blame her. It would be awful to be caught creeping by daylight!

I always lock the door when I creep by daylight. I can't do it at night, for I know John would suspect something at once.

And John is so strange now. I don't want to upset him. I wish he would take another room! Besides, I don't want anybody to get that woman out at night but myself.

\* \* \*

If only that top pattern could be gotten off from the one underneath! I mean to try it, little by little.

There are only two more days to get this paper off. I believe John is beginning to notice. I don't like the look in his eyes.

He has asked me all sorts of questions, too. Of course he was pretending to be very loving and kind. As if I couldn't see through him!

* * *

Hurrah! This is the last day, but it is enough. John is to stay in town overnight.

I made good progress last evening. As soon as there was moonlight, that poor woman began to crawl and shake the pattern. I got up and ran to help her.

I pulled and she shook. I shook and she pulled. Before morning, we had peeled off yards of that awful paper.

We got rid of a strip about as high as my head and half around the room.

The next morning, Jennie looked at the wall in amazement. She said that I shouldn't make myself tired. She said that *she* would peel the paper off if it bothered me all that much.

But I am here, and no one touches this paper but me—not *alive!*

Jennie tried to get me out of the room. But I told her it was so quiet now that I thought I would take a nap. So now she is gone. Most of our things have been moved, since we are leaving tomorrow. There is nothing left but that big bed. It is nailed down to the floor.

I quite enjoy the room, now that it is bare again.

How those children did tear about here!

The bed is really chewed up!

But I must get to work.

I have locked the door and thrown the key outside.

I don't want to go out. And I don't want to have anybody come in till John gets home.

I want to surprise him.

I have a rope up here that even Jennie did not find. If that woman in the wallpaper does get out and tries to get away, I can tie her!

But I forgot that I could not reach far without anything to stand on!

The bed will *not* move!

I tried to lift it and push it until I felt weak. Then I got so angry I bit off a little piece at one corner. But it hurt my teeth.

I am getting angry enough now to jump out of the window. It would be good exercise—but the bars are too strong even to try.

Besides, I wouldn't do it. Of course not. I don't even like to *look* out of the windows. There are too many of those creeping women out there, and they creep so fast.

I wonder if they all come out of that wallpaper as I did?

But I am firmly tied now by my well-hidden rope. You won't get *me* out in the road there!

I suppose I shall have to get back behind the pattern when night comes— and that is hard! It is so pleasant to be out in this great, empty room and creep around as I please!

I don't want to go outside. I won't, even if Jennie asks me to. Outside, you have to creep on the ground. And everything there is green instead of yellow. But here I can creep smoothly on the floor. My shoulder just fits in that long mark around the wall, so I cannot lose my way.

Why, there's John at the door!

It is no use, young man, you can't open it!

How he does call and pound!

Now he's crying for an axe.

It would be a shame to break down that beautiful door!

"John, dear!" I said in a gentle voice. "The key is down by the front steps, under a leaf."

And then I said it again, several times, very slowly. At last he had to go and see. Finally he got the key, of course, and came in. He stopped short by the door.

"What is the matter?" he cried. "For God's sake, what are you doing!"

I kept on creeping just the same, but I looked at him over my shoulder.

"I've got out at last," I said, "in spite of you and Jennie. And I've pulled off most of the paper, so you can't put me back!"

Now why should that man have fainted? But he did, and right across my path by the wall. Now I have to creep over him every time!

# The Widow's Might

Can you ever be sure that you "know what's best" for someone else? In this story three grown children return home for their father's funeral. They can't agree on who should take care of their mother. It never occurs to them that the widow might have plans of her own.

"WELL," SAID JAMES A LITTLE TOO QUICKLY. "WHAT
ARE WE GOING TO DO WITH MOTHER?"

# The Widow's Might

James had come to the funeral, but his wife, Maude, had not. She could not possibly leave the children. At least, that's what James said to everyone. The real reason was that his wife never wanted to leave New York—except for Europe or for summer vacations. A trip to Denver to attend a funeral was not her idea of fun.

Ellen and Adelaide were both there. Of course they felt that they had to come. But their husbands had not. Mr. Jennings could not leave his classes in Cambridge. Mr. Oswald could not leave his business in Pittsburgh. That is what they said.

The last services were over. The two sisters and their brother had had a cold, sad lunch. All of them were going to take the night train home again. Now they were waiting for the lawyer. He was coming at four o'clock to read the will.

"It's just something that has to be done. There can't be much money left," said James.

"No," agreed Adelaide. "I suppose not."

"A long illness eats up everything," said Ellen with a sigh. She knew, because her husband had come to Colorado for his lungs years ago. His health was still not very good.

"Well," said James a little too quickly. "What are we going to do with Mother?"

"Well, of course," Ellen began, "we *could* take her with us. It would depend a good deal on how much money is left, I suppose. I mean, it would depend on where she wants to go. Edward's salary is more than needed now." Ellen's thoughts seemed a little mixed up.

"She can come with me if she'd rather do that, of course," said Adelaide. "But I don't think she'd like it. Mother never did like Pittsburgh."

James looked from one to the other.

"Let me see—how old is Mother?"

"Oh, she's all of 50," answered Ellen. "And she's very upset, I think. It's been a long strain, you know." She turned to her brother. "I should think *you* could make her more comfortable than either of us, James. You have such a big house."

"I think a woman is always happier living with a son than with a daughter's husband," said Adelaide. "I've always thought so."

"That is often true," said James. "But it depends." He stopped speaking, and the sisters looked at each other. They knew what it depended upon.

"Perhaps if she stayed with me, you could—help some," said Ellen.

"Of course, of course, I could do that," he said. It was clear that he would rather send money than have his mother live with him. "She might visit between the two of you—take turns. And I could pay her expenses. About how much do you think that would be? We might as well get everything taken care of while we're all here."

"Things cost a lot these days," Ellen said. "But of course it would be only just *what* it costs. I wouldn't want to *make* anything."

"It's work and care, Ellen, and you may as well say so," said Adelaide. "You need all your strength, with those sickly children and Edward on your hands. If she comes to me, there would be no cost, James. Except for clothes. I have enough room, and Mr. Oswald will never notice the difference in the house bills. But he does hate to pay out money for clothes."

"Well, Mother must be taken care of properly," the son said. "How much per year would it cost for clothes?"

"You know what your wife's clothes cost," said Adelaide with a smile.

"Oh, *no*. You can't compare the two!" said Ellen. "Maude is in society. Mother wouldn't *dream* of having so much."

James smiled at her, as if to say thank you. "Board and clothes, all told—what would you say, Ellen?"

Ellen looked in her small black handbag for a piece of paper, but she found none. James handed her an envelope and a pen.

"Food these days costs about four dollars a week for one person," she said. "And then there's heat and light bills. I think six a week would be the *least*, James. And then she would need clothes and pocket money. I would say—well, $600 a year for everything."

"How about Oswald helping out with that, Adelaide?"

Adelaide got a little red in the face. "I do not think that he would be willing to, James. Of course, if it were really needed—"

"He has enough money," said her brother.

"Yes, but he never seems to have any extra. He has his own parents to support now. No—I can give her a home, but that's all."

"You see, you'd have none of the care and trouble, James," said Ellen. "We, the girls, are each willing to have her with us. I don't think your wife would want to. If you could just pay the money—"

"Maybe there is some money left, after all," said Adelaide. "And this place of hers might sell for something."

"This place" was a stretch of rolling land about 10 miles from Denver. It reached all the way up to the foothills. A river ran through it, and there was a view of the Rocky Mountains to the west. To the east were views of the plains.

"It should be worth at least six or eight thousand dollars," said James.

"Speaking of clothes," said Adelaide, changing the topic. "I see that Mother didn't buy a new black dress for the funeral. And she's always worn black, as long as I can remember."

"Mother's been upstairs a long time," said Ellen. "I'll go see if she wants anything."

"No," said Adelaide. "She told me she wanted to be left alone to rest. Let her be. She said she'd be down by the time Mr. Frankland got here."

"She seems to be taking it pretty well," said Ellen, after a little silence.

"It's not like a broken heart," Adelaide said. "Of course, Father meant well—"

"He was a man who always did his duty," said Ellen. "But I can't say that any of us really *loved* him very much."

"He is dead and buried," said James with a frown. "We can at least show some respect and not talk like that."

"We've hardly seen Mother, under that black veil," Ellen said. "It must have aged her—taking care of him for so long."

"She had some help toward the end— a male nurse," said Adelaide.

"Yes, but a long illness is always very difficult. And Mother never was very good at nursing. She has surely done her duty," said Ellen.

"And now she deserves a rest," said James, standing up and walking around the room. "I wonder how soon we can get rid of this place. There might be enough money in it to take care of her."

Ellen looked out across the dusty land.

"How I hated to live here!" she said.

"So did I," said Adelaide.

"So did I," said James.

They all smiled rather grimly.

"We don't seem to be very loving about Mother," Adelaide said with a touch of shame in her voice. "I don't know why it is. We never were a loving family, I guess."

"Nobody could be loving with Father," said Ellen.

"And Mother—poor Mother! I'm afraid she's had an awful life."

"Mother has always done her duty," said James. "And so did Father—as he saw it. Now we'll do ours."

"Ah," exclaimed Ellen. "Here comes the lawyer. I'll call Mother."

She ran upstairs and knocked at her mother's door.

"Mother, oh Mother," she cried. "Mr. Frankland's here."

"I know it," answered a voice from within. "Tell him to go ahead and read the will. I'll be down soon."

Ellen went back downstairs and told the others what her mother had said.

"That's quite natural," Mr. Frankland said, "under the circumstances. Sorry I couldn't get to the funeral. I had to appear in court this morning."

The will was short. First it said that the children's mother, if she were still living, would get half. Then the rest was to be divided among the children in four equal parts. Two parts would go to the son and one each to the daughters. The children were then directed to take care of their mother while she lived.

The estate was made up of the ranch, and the large house on it—with all the furniture, animals, and farm tools. There was also five thousand dollars in mining stocks.

"That is less than I expected," said James. He frowned at the lawyer as if it were his fault.

"This will was made 10 years ago," said Mr. Frankland. "I have done business for your father ever since that time. He was in sound mind until the end. I think you will find that there may be a little more. Your mother has taken excellent care of the ranch, I understand. She has even had some boarders."

The sisters gave each other pained looks.

"There's an end to all that now," said James.

Just then, the door opened. A tall figure, dressed in black and wearing a veil, came into the room.

"I'm glad to hear you say that Mr. McPherson was in sound mind until the end. It's true. I didn't come down to hear that old will. It's no good now."

They all turned in their chairs.

"Is there a later will, madam?" asked the lawyer.

"Not that I know of. Mr. McPherson had no property when he died."

"No property! But my dear lady—four years ago he certainly had some."

"Yes, but three and a half years ago he gave it all to me. Here are the deeds."

And there they were, in her hand— correct, simple, and clear. James R.

McPherson, Sr., had given his wife the whole estate. The deeds were all in order.

"You remember there was some trouble that year," she said. "Mr. McPherson thought he might lose the land. That is why he put it in my name. He thought it would be safer that way."

"Why, yes," said Mr. Frankland. "I do remember now that he asked me what I thought about it. I told him I didn't think the step was necessary."

James cleared his throat.

"Well, Mother, this *does* change things a little. We were hoping that we could finish this business today, with Mr. Frankland's help. Then we thought we'd take you back with us."

"We can't stay away from our homes any longer, you see, Mother," said Ellen.

"Can't you just deed it back again, Mother?" said Adelaide. "You could put it in James's name—or in all of our names—so we can get away."

"Why should I?" the tall woman asked in a steady voice.

"Now, Mother," said Ellen, "we know how badly you feel. You are nervous and tired. But I told you this morning that we wanted to take you back with us. I know you've been packing—"

"Yes, I've been packing," said the voice behind the veil.

"I am sure you were wise, Mother, to have the property put in your name," said James. "But now I think it would be best for you to deed it to me. I will see to it that Father's wishes are carried out to the letter."

"Your father is dead," said the voice.

"Yes, Mother, we know. We know how you feel," said Ellen.

"*I* am alive," said Mrs. McPherson.

"Dear Mother, it's very hard to talk business at such a sad time," said Adelaide. "But when we got here, we told you we couldn't stay long."

"And the business has to be settled," said James.

"It *is* settled," said the voice behind the veil.

"Perhaps Mr. Frankland can make it clear to you," continued James.

"I think that your mother sees everything quite clearly," said Mr. Frankland with a small smile. "I have always found her to be a very intelligent woman."

"Thank you, Mr. Frankland. Perhaps you can make my children understand that this property is mine now."

"Why, surely, surely, Mrs. McPherson," the lawyer said. "We all see that. But your children want you to think of Mr. McPherson's wishes concerning the estate."

"I have thought of Mr. McPherson's wishes for 30 years," she said. "Now, I'll think of my own. I have done my duty since the day I married him. It is eleven thousand days—today." She said the last with great force.

"But madam, your children—"

"I have no children, Mr. Frankland. I have two daughters and a son. These grown persons here *were* my children. Now they are grown up and married, with children of their own. I did my duty by them, and they did their duty by me. They would keep on doing so, I am sure." Her tone of voice changed suddenly. "But they don't have to. I'm tired of duty."

The little group looked up, surprised.

"You don't know how things have been going on here," the voice went on. "I didn't trouble you with any of it. But I'll tell you now. When your father put the property in my name—to save it—I took hold of things. I had to get a nurse for your father. A doctor came to visit quite often.

"The house became a sort of hospital— and I made it a little more so. I had six patients and nurses here, and I made some money by it. I ran the garden, kept the cows, and raised the chickens. I worked outdoors and even slept outdoors sometimes. I am a stronger woman today than I ever was in my life!"

She stood up, tall, strong, and straight. She took a deep breath.

"Your father's property was worth about eight thousand dollars when he died. After I take my share, that would give two thousand dollars to James and one thousand to each of the girls. I'm willing to give that to you now, in your own names.

"But if my daughters will listen to me, I'd like to tell them something. It would be better if I would send them the income from the money each year, in cash. They could spend it as they like. Otherwise, their husbands will take it. It is good for a woman to have some money of her own."

"I think you are right, Mother," said Adelaide quickly.

"Yes, indeed," said Ellen.

"Don't you need it yourself, Mother?" asked James. He suddenly had a feeling of tenderness for the figure in black.

"No, James. I shall keep the ranch, you see. I have good help. So far I've made two thousand dollars a year from the ranch. Now I've rented it for that amount to a friend of mine."

"I think you've done quite well, Mrs. McPherson," said the lawyer in surprise.

"And you'll have an income of two thousand a year," said Adelaide, as if she could hardly believe it.

"You'll come and live with me, won't you?" asked Ellen eagerly.

"No, dear, I will not," her mother replied.

"You're *more* than welcome in my big house," said Adelaide.

"No, thank you, my dear."

"I am sure Maude would be glad to have you with us," said James.

"I am sure that she would *not*, James. No, thank you, my dear."

"But what *are* you going to do?" Ellen seemed to be quite concerned.

"I'm going to do what I never did before. I'm going to *live!*"

With a strong, fast step, the tall figure moved to the windows and opened the shades. The bright Colorado sunshine poured into the room. She threw off the long black veil.

"I borrowed that veil," she said. "I didn't want to hurt your feelings at the funeral."

Then she unbuttoned the long black cloak and dropped it at her feet. She stood there in the full sunlight, smiling. She was wearing a well-made traveling suit of beautiful mixed colors.

"If you want to know my plans, I'll tell you. I have six thousand dollars of my own. I earned it in three years—from my little ranch-hospital. I put one thousand dollars in the bank. That is to bring me back from anywhere on earth.

"There will still be enough to put me in an old ladies' home, if you have to. Here is an agreement with a cremation company. They'll bring my body home, if necessary, and have me cremated—or they don't get the money. But I've got five thousand dollars to play with, and I'm going to play."

Her daughters looked shocked.

"Why, Mother—"

"At your age—"

The frown on James's face turned into a scowl. He looked like his father.

"I knew that none of you would understand," she went on in a quiet tone. "But it doesn't matter anymore. I gave you 30 years—you and your father. Now I'll have 30 of my own."

"Are you sure you're well, Mother?" Ellen asked.

Her mother laughed out loud.

"Well, really well, never was better. I have been doing business up to today. That's proof enough that I am quite well. I want you to understand that your mother is a Real Person. She has interests of her own and half a lifetime left.

"The first 20 years didn't count for much. I was growing up then and could do little to help myself. And the last 30 years have been hard. Perhaps James understands that more than you girls—but you all know it. Now, I'm free."

"Where *do* you mean to go, Mother?" James asked.

"To New Zealand. I've always wanted to go there," she said. "Now I'm going. And to Australia, and Tasmania, and Madagascar, and Tierra del Fuego. I shall be gone for quite some time."

The McPherson family separated that night. Three went east, and one went west.

# Mr. Peebles' Heart

Is it possible to give so much to others that you have nothing left for yourself? In this story, a worn-out man finds that a little selfishness is just what the doctor ordered.

SHE TOLD HER SISTER THAT SHE DIDN'T HAVE TO LISTEN
TO THE MUSIC IF SHE DIDN'T WANT TO.

# Mr. Peebles' Heart

He was lying on the sofa in the bare little sitting room. It wasn't a comfortable sofa, but there was room enough to stretch out on it. Mr. Peebles was sound asleep. It was a hot, still afternoon. The only sound in the room was a soft little snore from time to time.

Mrs. Peebles had gone off on some errands. She had asked her sister Joan to come along.

"You must meet people if you're going to live in this town," Mrs. Peebles had said. "You should take an interest in the club, it seems to me."

"I'm going to live here as a doctor," Joan said, "not as a lady of leisure. You go on, Em. I'm happy here. I'll keep Arthur company when he wakes up."

So Mrs. Emma Peebles went on alone to the Ellsworth Ladies' Home Club. And Dr. J. R. Bascom quietly went into the sitting room to look for the book she was reading.

There was Mr. Peebles, still asleep. She sat down in a rocker by the window and looked at her brother-in-law. For a while she watched him, first as a doctor and then with a deeper human interest.

Arthur Peebles at 50 was becoming a bit bald, gray, and fat. He had a face that changed throughout the day. For customers, he always wore a friendly smile. But when there was no one to serve, there were deep, sad lines around the corners of his mouth. Mr. Peebles had always been a slave of duty.

If ever a man had done his duty—as he saw it—Arthur had done his, always.

His duty—the way he saw it—was to support women. First it was his mother.

She had been a strong and able person who had run the farm by herself after her husband's death. She had also added to their income by taking in summer boarders. Until Arthur was old enough to "support her," she had worked very hard. Then she had sold the farm and moved to town to "make a home for Arthur." Arthur, of course, had hired a helper to do most of the hard work of home-making.

Arthur worked in the store. His mother sat on the porch and talked with her neighbors.

He took care of his mother until he was nearly 30. Then he married and moved into his own house. His wife was a pretty, careless, clinging little thing. She had always depended on Arthur's strength. To this day, she continued to cling to him as if she could not do a thing for herself.

Both of their daughters were married in due time. In their turn, they had both found strong young husbands to cling to. Now Arthur Peebles had only his wife to support. It was the lightest load he had ever had, at least numerically. He had always thought it was a man's job to support women.

If Dr. Joan had needed his support, he would have cheerfully added her to the list. He liked her very much. She was different from any woman he had ever known. She was as different from her sister as day was from night.

Joan Bascom had left home at an early age, against her mother's will. Some people in town thought she had run away with a man. But the truth was that she had only gone off to college. She worked her way through. First she became a trained nurse. Then later she studied medicine, and had long ago become a doctor. Now there were stories that she must be "pretty well fixed" and ready to "retire." Other stories said that she must have failed in some way. Why else would she have come back home to live?

Whatever the reason, she was there, a welcome visitor. Her sister was proud of her, and her brother-in-law was glad to have her company.

As Joan watched him sleep, she thought about what a *good* man he was. Then one of his arms dropped, and his hand hit the floor. With a start, his eyes opened and he sat up quickly.

"Don't sit up that fast, Arthur. It's bad for your heart."

"Nothing is the matter with my heart, is there?" he asked, smiling.

"I don't know. I haven't examined it. Now, sit still. You know there's nobody in the store this afternoon. And if there is, Jake can wait on them."

"Where's Emma?"

"Oh, Emma's gone to her club or something. She wanted me to go along, but I'd rather talk with you."

He looked pleased but unbelieving. Arthur Peebles had a high opinion of the club, but a low one of himself. He poured himself a cold drink and moved into another rocker.

"Look here," she said. "What would you *like* to do if you could?"

"Travel!" said Mr. Peebles. He saw how surprised she was. "Yes, travel! I've always wanted to, ever since I was a kid. No use! We never could, you see. And now—even if we could—Emma hates it." He sighed gently.

"Do you like keeping the store?" she asked.

"*Like* it?" He smiled at her, but with a hopeless look just behind the smile. "No, not really, Joan. Not even a little bit. But so what?"

There was silence for a while, and then she asked another question. "What work would you have liked to do, if you had been free to choose?"

His answer surprised her, partly because it was so fast. He blurted out just one word—"Music!"

"When I was a child," he told her, "Father brought home a guitar. He said it was for the one who learned to play it first. He meant the girls, of course. As a matter of fact, *I* learned it first—but I didn't get it.

"That's all the music I ever had," he added. "And there's not much to listen to here, except what they play in church. I'd get a record player, but Emma says she'd smash it. She says that records sound worse than cats. People have different tastes, you know, Joan."

Again he smiled at her. He said, "Well, I must be getting back to the store."

A few days later, Joan was talking to her sister. "Emma," she said, "how would you like it if I moved in here instead of getting my own place?"

"I was hoping that you would," said her sister.

"Do you think Arthur would like it?"

"Of course he would! Besides, even if he didn't—you're *my* sister, and this is *my* house. He put it in my name a long, long time ago."

"I see," said Joan, "I see." Then after a moment, she said to her sister, "Emma, are you happy?"

"Happy? Why, of course I am." Then Mrs. Peebles listed all the things she was thankful for. Among those things, she did not even mention Arthur. She didn't seem to think of him at all. Then Dr. Joan asked what she thought of the state of his health.

"His health? Arthur's? Why, he's always well. Never had a sick day in his life. Except, now and then, he's had a kind of a breakdown," she added as an afterthought.

\* \* \*

Before long Dr. Joan Bascom became quite comfortable in the little town. She soon took over the practice of old Dr. Braithwaite and made a few friends. Her sister and her brother-in-law enjoyed having her live with them. "There's plenty of room now that the girls are gone," they told her.

Once her own life was in order, Dr. Joan began a secret campaign. She set out to help her brother-in-law get more joy out of *his* life.

Her first step was to buy a good record player and a set of first-class records. With a smile, she told her sister that she didn't have to listen if she didn't want to. At first Emma would sit, a bit angry, in the back room, while her husband and sister enjoyed the music. But then she grew used to it and sat closer. She might, for example, sit on the porch. In any case, Arthur was finally able to enjoy his music in peace.

The music seemed to stir something in him. As the music played he would rise and walk about the house with a new fire in his eyes. Dr. Joan fed that fire with talk and books and pictures. She would often show him maps and descriptions of sailing tours.

"I don't see what you two find so interesting about music," Emma would say. Arthur never argued with her. He just got quiet and lost that sparkle in his eye when she talked about it.

Then one day, when Emma was at the club, Dr. Joan made a bold attack.

"Arthur," she said, "do you trust me as a doctor?"

"I would rather go to you than to any doctor I ever saw," he answered.

"Will you let me prescribe something for you if I tell you that you need it?"

"I sure will."

"Will you *take* the prescription?"

"Of course I will—no matter how it tastes!"

"Very well. I prescribe two years in Europe."

He stared at her in shock.

"I mean it," she said. "Your condition is more serious than you think. I want you to get away from here. I want you to travel. For not less than two years."

He could only stare. "But Emma—"

"Never mind about Emma. She owns the house. She's got enough money to take care of herself. And I'm paying enough rent to keep everything going. Emma doesn't need you."

"But the store—"

"Sell the store."

"Sell it! That's easy to say. Who would buy it?"

"I will. Yes—I mean it. It should be worth seven or eight thousand dollars, stock and all?"

He nodded his head yes.

"Well, I'll buy it. You can live in Europe for two years on a couple of thousand. Then you'll have five thousand or so to come home to. When you come back, you can invest in something better than that shop. Will you do it?"

He quickly came up with a list of reasons why he couldn't.

She answered each one. "Nonsense! You can go! She doesn't need you at all. She may later. No, the girls don't need you, either. They may later.

"Now is your time—*now*. You can spend a year in Germany, learn the language, go to the opera. You can take walking trips. See Switzerland, England, Scotland, Ireland, France, Belgium, Denmark. You can do a lot in two years."

He stared at her, fascinated but fearful.

"Why not? Why not be your own man for once in your life? Do what *you* want to—not what other people want you to!"

Arthur mumbled something about duty, but she had an answer for that, too.

"If ever a man on earth has done his duty, Arthur Peebles, you have. You took care of your mother when she was perfectly able to take care of herself. You took care of your sisters as well. Then your daughters. And now your wife. At present, Emma does not need you the least bit in the world."

"Now that's pretty strong," he said. "Emma would miss me—I know she'd miss me—"

Dr. Bascom looked at him with affection. "Believe me, Arthur," she said. "The best thing for Emma—and for you, too—would be for her to miss you, real hard."

"I know she'd never let me go," he said.

"That's the good thing about having me here," she said. "You have a right to choose your doctor, don't you? And your doctor says that you *need* this. She is prescribing travel, rest, change, and music."

"But Emma—"

"Now, Arthur Peebles, forget Emma for a while. I'll take care of her. And let me tell you another thing—a change like this will do *her* good."

He stared at her, puzzled.

"I mean it. Having you away will give her a chance to stand on her own. Your letters about those places will interest her. She may even wish that she were traveling herself. Try it. Don't even talk it over with her. That will just cause trouble.

"Write up the papers for the sale of the store. I'll write you a check, and you can take the next boat for England. Once you're on board you can make the rest of your plans. Here's the address of a bank that will take care of your letters and checks—"

The thing was done! Arthur was gone before Emma had time to argue about it. The day Arthur left, she said to her sister, "But how do you think it *looks,* Joan? What will people think of me? To be left deserted like this!"

"What people think will depend on what you tell them—and how you act, Emma Peebles! Just say that Arthur was not well, and that I advised him to take a trip. Everything will be fine. Forget about yourself for once. Show some feelings for him."

For her own sake, Emma did what her sister told her. Yes, Arthur had gone to Europe for his health. Yes, Dr. Bascom was worried about him—chance of a complete breakdown, she said. Yes, the doctor had hurried him off. He was in England taking a walking trip. She did not know when he'd be back. The store? He'd sold it.

Dr. Bascom hired someone who was much more interested in the store than Mr. Peebles had been. She turned it into a good paying business.

Arthur was a new man by the time he returned home. But Emma had changed the most. With talk, with books, and with trips to see her daughters, she had grown more independent. When she got letters from Arthur, she followed his trip on maps. She took in a boarder or two "for company." One way and another, she grew stronger and more interesting.

Arthur left behind an unhappy, boring woman who clung to him as if he were a beast of burden. He returned to a woman who had changed for the better. Now that she had feet of her own to stand on, she was much happier with life—and with him.

Arthur looked like a different person. The stoop was gone from his shoulders. The sad lines around his eyes had disappeared. Both his mind and his body were refreshed and active. He had found himself.

And he found her again, too. The next time he got the urge to travel, Emma thought she'd go, too. She turned out to be a very pleasant companion, and the two of them took many enjoyable trips together.

But neither of them could ever get Dr. Bascom to name the disease that Mr. Peebles had suffered from. "A dangerous heart condition" was all she would tell them. When he said he had no such trouble now, she said that it had "responded to treatment."

# Thinking About
# the Stories

## The Yellow Wallpaper

1. Some stories are packed with action. In other stories, the key events take place in the minds of the characters. Is this story told more through the characters' thoughts and feelings? Or is it told more through their outward actions?

2. Compare and contrast at least two characters in this story. In what ways are they alike? In what ways are they different?

3. Good writing always has an effect on the reader. How did you feel when you finished reading this story? Were you surprised, horrified, amused, sad, touched, or inspired? What elements in the story made you feel that way?

The Widow's Might

1. The plot is the series of events that takes place in a story. Usually, story events are linked in some way. Can you name an event in this story that was the cause of a later event?

2. Who is the main character in this story? Who are one or two of the minor characters? Describe each of these characters in one or two sentences.

3. Is there a character in this story who makes you think of yourself or someone you know? What did the character say or do to make you think that?

Mr. Peebles' Heart

1. An author builds the plot around the conflict in a story. In this story, what forces or characters are struggling against each other? How is the conflict finally resolved?

2. All the events in a story are arranged in a certain order, or sequence. Tell about one event from the beginning of this story, one from the middle, and one from the end. How are these events related?

3. Is there a hero in this story? A villain? Who are they? What did these characters do or say to form your opinion?

8